THRUM

Also by Natalie Simpson

accrete or crumble

Each leaf a runnel the

roofs now skiffs in green

I've never done anything

but begin.

– Lisa Robertson, *the weather*

CONTENTS

The poem trails the typing hand. The hand creases and clatters. The fingers jumble twitching. The poem defies corrosion. The hand defiles the poem. The poem clothes the hand.

ENUNCIATION OF THE FERVOUR

Sentencing

Faking out graciously. Fake would have numerics stop.

Fog short. Fog. Short hop.

Sodden twos and threes cling string bed of growing hoard for further distribution.

A partly hidden partly able parted red.

Rush a bead through beaded through better half broken half a leg-shake.

Break certain through brick stands sent reason to rouse a small flag flutter.

Wings would shudder.

Arisen single syncopate.

Single single syncopate.

Soon he wedded cold and striking.

He stands at barn side sing.

His turn, word burns, he break, rope sick, scald.

Sick of it, basting, he lettered.

See bending in knee or knowledge pending grip pending gather.

Thrust this. Thrift tryst.

A must.

Form simple scintillate. Simple sin tolls.

Sax.

(Sentence is a word in pieces, plastered, faster.)

The reluctant two some time has a future present. Tense or tense now keen through shoulder blades dull ache neighbours.

Gone a wail thin gutter undertones gather my mouth is a-brick with feeling.

One had fearing one had felt.

I'm afraid: it's rhythm. Has tone down has two tone has tricks at the stop and the stick.

Ballad of a Leaden Moment

Elaborate sapped antidote.

Torrid engagement burns.

Top to bottom, ankles to eyelids.

Tobacco simmers a clutch.

Addendum in code.

Forays into fastenings.

Button, zip.

Lip up.

Enter philatelist :: scenes set in absurdity seldom fruition or flower. Allow for any occurrence or regret. Numb and chill the ego blackens and storms find refuge – let notices let flop. "I would be a whore for a word." Or a song. Where do stamps fit, "I ask you." A faulty construction. I will crumble into you/or onto. Enter the rubble or a fine dust. Let style.

Two

… overhead

he glowers politely

at least well met in thinking

love will regret me

  let me

regress into desire

fretful in minor episodes

      or strung

a tuning fork carnality

a simple line

of dust and ashes breeze

by, marking

   one or one too many

  flames on tongue

on spoken

 long for

he cried.

Notes

Language is speech less speaking.

> – Ferdinand de Saussure

Back onto excess with tentativity. Work at the great numb.

Language is a likely state. A limb drug flopping.

One plus one synchronically. Language and the ever addition.
Logos got good.

Whoever said a certain letter said letters into infinity. Whoever set
my arbitrary bonded me.

I have clause for bonding leagues beyond me.

Said hedonist whoever said this letter licks. Whoever form and fashion
form fast.

Every body participates in language all the time. Alliterati in perpetuity. Perpetual machination.

More to the rhythm of your harness time and harping struck. The strain you surely. A state of excitability flutters with weak descriptors.

Language is powerless in this shift.

A Long and Fitful Sentence Accumulating Grace

And during the period of twenty-one years from my death if the said Lilian Aspinall shall live so long to accumulate the surplus if any of such income at compound interest by investing the same and the resulting income thereof in any of the investments aforesaid by way of addition to the capital of such fund as aforesaid and so as to be subject to the same trusts as are hereby declared concerning the same and during the remainder of the life of the said Lilian Aspinall in case she shall survive the said period of twenty-one years to pay or apply such surplus income (if any) to the person or persons or for the purposes to whom and for which the same would for the time being be payable or applicable if the said Lilian Aspinall were then dead.

Re Smith [1928] Ch 915

Of Geographic Interiors

Adrift and plainsong tasked with swim. In which they meadow, in which they stall blame.

Lock sought click.
Lip caught stain.

The precious game lumps. The sweet men mind themselves. They brain calamity.

Roaming authorly, stitching shambles. To have overly strewn one's petals. To have thrown oneself into blank rot.

Of stone and stack. Of interstices granulate.

To have traumatized one's only scale.

Each gathering weathering interrupt. Fluted hewing.

Seeded sea. Balmy rooms. An inner weather. Solemn city.

Filter out and drip flimsy. Empty cloud sunk into its shedding. Empty cloud inconstituent.

In which they banter and crash. In which we they. In which they welter.

Having often tenuously, beautifully, murderously used.

What empty feathers into and infects.

We subject ourselves to identity and craft our unravelling, looped thread, tufted yarn, weave a plausible synthesis of impulses.

Form dense verb clusters, looted, lit, stung.

Grip tamps.
Frail pluck.

Tick bloom from sprung violets, tick potent.

We flay temperate, inconsequential, and waver. An atrocious scrimmage. A centre point. They have ripped fault exquisitely into ragged edge of nuance.

Strum lilting.

Whirr clip.

An inhabitation.

Hoarse infringement, rotoring clench. They porous root, they bolster.

ECHO LOCALIAL

Home is small bills. Packing 99 square feet.

Shale tight.   Shale slid.

          Eyelids by day.

And day all equations.

Equatorial new guinea, old soft shoe. Who bids?

          Why not try sampling?

These days are harpy.

Home is what engenders. Mulish aping shapes.

Slap. Hop. Proliferate.

          Spindle trim.

Grapple every filament twisting without wind.

So who? Tell now, time nags.

         Drapes askew.

Roughly woven, rough to touch.

Small words stalling fog. The rest are tongue-flicks.

       Home is how hard you eat your heart out.

Points of light flicker and burn in oxygenated sentiment.

Snuff once.

Sediment more

    faithfully records.

This side of the comma, this side of the comma.

Some kind of owl makes the news. Some kind of mental

breakdown trumps others.

Rub up slip shudders.

Shipyard, flames. Dark surges. Hobbled loose to lame.

Fluently corrupt tongues hang tidy lines. Headless seeks same. Born to redress. Feathered slattern. Cut to cloth bolt humming.

Thrum sticks firm into firm place. Subordinate rhythm save reason. Laid face to lathe.

Cacophony incarcerated.

Cinder footnotes link bush and valley, text and territorial vein. Who gathers prairie thistles, dust dry or bone bent.

Set a caustic interlude to crash. A bare promise mutilates. Steam runs to still. An agreeable same trick.

Home is what rivets.

I've found a door which lets me out. Or at least tugging handle.

So, I thought, why not, try writing. A head injury not with standing.

Every day knows the tune.

       Dam the hours.

Lapwing sounds fluttery. An evil birdish. Nobody inhabits white.

Surface correlates. The coarse grain trains the eye
leftward to pocks.

Adrift and spinning. Sumptuous bursts. Burgundy hem. Satin
coat lining.

These fine unmistakable.

Lapwing sounds clumsy.

Thunderous flapping.

Sensual and digital, muttering fingers.

Callous cold aster.   Stamen and lisp.

Edificial thrum. Cusp up. Shrug after shrug.

                    Make no mistake.

Heard teeth clink.

Heard crates grate.

Who adheres here? Who hopes the most?

Home is where the stakes get stuck. Home

is where the damp creeps.

A red sash. Now I'm crafted. A real plush run.

Home comes flippant.   Every day bests.

          Snow sits all week on trees.

The clod plods come-ons. Clocked solid. Shoes bleed black.

                                        Hack.

Home is loose noosing.

Word and stop.   ˙

          My artistic clap.

Atone. Trip the light maraudic. Dive off.

Some trucks blather past.

A home is trying.

O blind, formidable.

Apology forks.

Once a day fell through. Surely all kinds of events reverberate.

Reciprocal simmerings, fade to beating. Light fails to nuance.

Pressured sanction.

Word a pearl.

Punitive measures a second. Legs a-gashing. Into which.

Plum custom.

A pertinent detail in my perambulation.

Sweet trees. Sheets and shes. Saucy cant.

Each a fallow.

Row home.

JACK STATE

Climates facilitate ennui.

Here and here and herer.

Vallarta

Terrible moments, these. Nothing to do
and must write. Pelicans swim the sea
and please. The land is a light and
falters. Flickers. False as old fortuna this
problem of poetry.

If a sentence streams a sea of thought,
then can it end. At the breakers or
their force the beach in a straight line.
If a sentence has streaming, is
streamlined, if a sentence is lined, it
lies. Thinks of a grid and this is a
grid. Rid of a buzzing or old
structures carapace.

Stream a river not a sea but see this is
the ocean become my circumstance and
frame. Only the sea leaks into the
poetry should be luscious but dry
cracking calgary words don't want to
recede. Receive a slow-and-easy sensuality
cosmo is gust for the mill.

And the *costumer* is always wrong.

So the geckos, and black birds look
up for their living and isn't it
ridicarus circling the sun in a
misplaced metaphor under a spanish
sun melting words are heard as in
busto for *gusto* my *cabellos* are curly
my whys and wherefores are *por.*

Nineteen

symptoms at breakfast at nerve porridge

push bedrooms push fact

pretty Shakespeare funk

old half found

all boots and headaches

worked a pretty comb

old fool pocked and married

talked stone six

talked street wretch

Forty-One

upstairs handsome

dropped old days

sad floor Sally

loved click handle

      gush and burning crocus

floor click   lit house

      falling love split

gush pour thick skin

      swore thin   blush check

often not often

handle on the verge

Stick

I'd like to loosen your tight wad was lasting all my faster aspects.

Ponder the heft of language less each book end borders this break.

Black and blister you simplistic stutter you utter fine at a time like this.

My heavy muted under humid a negative form of the verb I have done wrong.

Spread a beautiful landscape.

Strange bent of mind seeks straightening.

Perpetual moments thin into lengths of beat and lashing.

Take sand down to seashore for the futility.

Things mean here, the guard is down, lit cracks, gravity steps.

I have achieved intention.

Break out of your shall.

No Code Means

Are you both car and driver? Unsubstantiated?

Shifting?

ASSUME SILENCE BUT LOW PITCHES

inescapably

He applies skills, suckling. They are never amusing. Minute – *oot* – scabary: the leaded middle. Fingers in sockets and pudding.

My present present tastes of iron. Tang. bone sidling bone.

metasensual senses the sense of

lopes and fallows

magnetic storm syndrome

legs buckle arms loop

Time comes to pester.

                                        (a plausible wanting odds

Splice this vision into that   deafens –

This terminology flies or flat   apple-cheek wanton

                                          dear and feminite

                                          fame and laminate

Morning dregs: coarse

reactionary fondles

Smoking ferocious, mortar shock and shill –

Thrilling

tonal –

cunning –

cataractic spans lexicon dam

NO CODE MEANS

(mainly syntax snatches

My Biography

What place is this, morning hovering, sky heavy, the guarded air. We were looking a foolish lull. Scraping pigeons. Seabird call. Trenchant scrags, the lush green trees.

The very air is breathing. City of lung.

(Today I have read that the family is a crisis the justice system is failing, that the federation is fragile but bound in doctrines, that the dust kicked up is falling in fanciful curlicues across shafts of light. *[I want to be wounded by words but itch more like touched nerves or sweat glands.]

Today I have bathed in light only I haven't today I stood in spring rain to smoke today I have lazed and sternly scolded my habits. Today I have not resisted closure and not resisted angst. [Typing {I don't understand this censure}.])

BOOK OF ECLECTIC SENTENCES

How are my wife and I supposed to understand Elvish?

The melancholy genius is left unaccounted for, as is the manic airhead.

What would tourists think of a habitat of denuded trees with desperate, starving koalas roaming the damaged landscape?

Why are there so many wallabies, and only one lion?

You'd get laid if you were a rodeo clown.

Has your dad ever not got his crop off in the fall?

Must be 18 over or older to order drink an alcoholic drinks.

Your aesthetics won't help you now.

TOT SPARKS PLUNGE

Lucky the Tot Wasn't Tasered

terror tots aside airports need common-sense security tot fighting cancer
is fact of fundraiser stop the quills another tot in turmoil mom hits
cougar with cooler to save tot

Quebec tot cut in robbery bid endangering tot condemned truck invades
tot's bedroom cat cushions tot's plunge flap over naps angers parents of
Ottawa tots tot wanders out into the cold tot takes toy truck for ride tot
who suffered near-fatal fall out of hospital spare us the imperilled tots

dead tot's dad not normal court told Judd's ex says he knew tot not his
tiny tots' tunic big fashion tot's ride of terror nets mom nine months

dazzling pop production for tot's dad gets access to tot sired in loveless
pact tot conceived after dad denied aid tot banned by preschool over
peanuts tot implicated father trial told

extreme cold credited in tot's creek fall survival adopted tots arrive in Vancouver here's a little food for tot please tips for tots and older parents panic after tot trots from sleepover tot taken care of while teen mom gets taught

Tot-Bots, Stand By

tots' snoring a warning: study Crocs for tots in the Congo romance with a tot in tow tot's a cue-ball whiz dad uses tot as shield to avoid being tasered toys for tots declines talking Jesus dolls

teaching tactics to tots hot tot tip: keep it simple tots need grown-ups not grow ops

tot hit; spanker jailed kin pray for tractor mishap tot the poison in your tot's bottle? tiny tot takes a break tots take a tumble tot looks for little dog disappears

tot terror the mod tot aqua tot tots who tote tenacious tots twirling tots library salsa tots

attract tots with toys, then give them books tattoo tot in sleep cycle two tots have a ball tots in the hall high heels on teetering tots? keep tots off the treadmills text touts "tattoo tolerance" to tots tot discipline seminar set tot finds fossil find exciting tot flung from Indian train seat fight recovering disco dad leaves tot to shiver tot drove drunk mom home

EFFULGENCE: AN ETIQUETTE

Part 1

Parsimony breeds languor. Excess will never fail to penetrate the veil of squalour. Chaste pallor signals balance of the mind –

The rosier the cheek, the more freighted dire thought.

A formal loosening about the eye sockets, a muscular relinquishing, can counteract any measure of pleasure.

Go on in this vein, trilling, charter demure tongue.

Brute occasion,
syllabic weight.

Approach new feeling tacitly, boldly, as an equivocating loop.

Current opinion stakes courtesy to wit. Follow the flux closely. Make subtle adjustments to stay onside.

Take tiny steps, occur gratuitously. Humility may mask effulgence.

Bloom or permeate.

Opportunity will not announce itself.

Portents rarely flare.

Favour a cocked ear.

Fashion a future from careful gathering.

A fluent cache of humour and light outlasts any currency.

A trimmer stem bears firmer fruit.

Cast line wants only reeling.

Fluid comments absorb cleanly into the membranous surface of specious discourse. Better the snag –

Intrepid thinkers struggle to speak.

Infectious banter violates an orderly prognosis. Mapping a crowd is like binding dust.

Billows to safety. Release abreast inchoate cloud.

Form follows function furthers form. Essentializing cyclical tautologies. Flames fathoms fodder flusters flame. Cinders settle succour single cinder. Repeat.

Exacerbate gaily all contempt you may encounter.

> The spruce tree honing spindles;
> the mountain sloughing rock.

Punctuate solidity with minute pockets of vapid being, anguish, and doubt. In fostering the bleakest inclination, self reflexively nurtures true self.

> Deep currents orchestrate tenors of fluttering
> tendrils. Deep tenders filter archival crust. Dip
> tremors curve remnants or tensors. Drop consoles
> torque folders of cuspid. Droop mouldering flagons
> of rust.

Populate your memory with relatable stations. Naturally recurring obelisks.

You'll receive what your appearance deserves each moment. You'll calibrate platelets. Correct and adjust.

A version of Corinthian solitude –

This potent thrumming

This adamant bliss

Adjust.   Correct this.

Assize your permissive boundaries. Drive fence posts, string wire. Hemming will coalesce your desire. Condense and intensify. All longing permits exclusion.

Formidable returns gather like moss on a stagnant passion. Swift decision permeates conscious yearning with impregnable satisfaction.

The bloom will blush that much longer.

Sprinkle charm throughout your acquaintance. The unlikeliest allies meet any number of crises fortuitously.

Cast loose nets.

The caught thrive unaware.

Part 2

Expect affect, trash delirious.

Each fingertip lavishing each surface offers singular delight.

(Study touch, its open, its arming.)

Build archives to ballast, trash affect.

Pasting luminous chance to random

adhesion, plying less to relish more. Sweet

billowing, salty lockets.

Why not fake enterprise, cast fodder? Your imagination stakes your only
bond.

Time warps porous.

Stretch a day's length, luxuriate in its insistent tick.

Subtle encumbrances drain energy into small rivulets: trickle and seep. Ground water harbours venom.

Bald theory may bait erasure.

Smoothly churn regret.

The slick blade meets a deeper pulse.

Only longing settles no debts.

Fashion a likely demeanour:

testing electric waters, siphon sparks. Plant tooth flash, sly grin.

Gently effacing lip and quiver. Let in only glimmers.

Sharp flash, bitter wit.

Circumstance breeds suspicion. Murmuring spurious intuition leads to spent.

Why fault paltry episodes with significant intrigue? Spin substance from filament, rumour from flash.

Cotton wisps enervate an orderly disposition.

Hanging threads agitate grip.

A sense of unravelling – drifting – dangerously unconstrained – may strike at odd moments of observation.

Give these strikings no truck.

A calm mind creates its surrounding. Project out and filter nothing in.

Lend a kinder ear to your peers. Beaming one to one may mean becoming more attuned, more exactly animated toward harmonious colloquy.

Companions, after all, centre a sense of self securely. Stay middling.

Untimely confession spoils leisure. Deep feeling leaks and corrodes. Trust no instinct to relieve burden, crave no release.

No one needs your longing. No one knows your capacities.

Walls loom and sever. Skirt inner. Lap courtyards of your own diversion. Create lakes of burning precision.

Branches catch a willing cloth. You murder your very inversion.

Harsh reminders of propriety bead and slip.

Be porcelain, be
impervious.

SYSTEMS OF PLEASURE

Dear Poet,

You can colonize your reader's hope.

Desire puppets them. Twist their stringing. Muddle them. Tangle them. Skip their synaptic rhythm to your pulse.

You corporealize the lag that leaves them stranded. Your flood may visit their longing. They may yet yearn at your disposal.

Remember to capsize your reader's distinction – his sense of taste, her discerning pantomime. Burn in the flavour of their fortune. This reader you've trailed craves capture, lavishing, balm.

affect Alto

who fails here?

who flailing, sails flagging, burnt opus?

cushion the senses, wracked breath

who defers here?

gleaming in wreckage, leaden lung-weights

flimsy clung stupor

brow furrets, skin runnel

scrap

who fallacies?

trim fawnishly

slavering, brawnily, copious

bore hobbles, straints

sore gutted

formerly

who brickets, faceless, obdurate, and surplused?

sacked travesties

mortaring

pummel wash

boozer

who pleathers? who shins?

anchorite, creaming, who ferrets?

who parcels?

slung rampant

dedicating grotesquery

moored tuft

splain

humouring foresight

flecked tense

Her silk dress hugging her points

(her hips) (a crisis points) (a crisis point)

– misquoted from Carole Maso's *AVA*

her lips. her glimmer. silk lining. hidden. draped. for granted. her dressing. her drugged gender. slipped. peel liner from liner, from curtain, from grace. slip into grace with crisis. with decision. separate. through. slip through crisis with draping. with dripping. with thin liner, shower, curtain, membrane. permeate grace with her. colourless silk. threads intention. drape cloth as shimmer. drape shine. her colourless glimmer. addresses points. decipher with intention. pointed. glimmer. her hips. point to crisis. take shine and hug in. hug into points. take to billow. take to silk. drape efficiently. lining, billow, sharp, decipher. gender dresses. this decision renders. her drugged membrane. her droop. her lip shimmy. her drugged loop. shimmer wraps her hips, loops her crisis. a neat resolution. take hips to neat points, hoop to shine, her confusion. her draped in. her pointed refusal. neat train. her thoughts loop. her training. take shimmer for granted. shine colour. granted silk a colour. commit to visual. demur from. thread text. intention. decision drapes her. separate, bent. from points of crisis. from lip points. from looping.

Turn Away

Try to belie the imagination. Try to imagine a wrinkle, a bruise, a point of convergence.

Eliminate all memory. Proliferate scathing. Engender sound.

Sound as though touched. Rake nerve for encumbrance. Rail against and in favour and inconsistent strain.

Last, at long last, as the long, last light fades, a curtain raised, a half-mast circumstance.

Indeed the abstract flails and whimpers. Indeed the words are pocked.

To get at turn away. To touch here and touch there so slowly a vein awakes. In the long light sombre and glare light brutal, in the hazing day, tactile nuance forms a soft fog.

A soft fog is a fidgety slip into limber touch, the tongue lisping through the typing.

Here silence sounds blinking a grasp in tumult, slowly lapping so lapse.

A moth in the moonlight is a moth indoors.

– Gertrude Stein, *History or Messages from History*

Moth in dorsal spectrum:

colours finning spike.

Spent fanning. First grapples. Rooted indoors, fungal spread. A moth elision, a moth elated. Light stipples featherly. Soft-lit mothing. Indignant. In doving.

Coloured grey, gold highlights, lit pulse to mottle. Brown undertones deep flay. Pled moth, ranking layers, strips law from pale wing prints. Mothlined in soft powder, stray flakes engolding ground.

Flowing to meet a lit glass ends at.

Wrought iron is a wrinkled tudor, history comes to grip a long moment. Indoors meant moth draw. Light filters simply.

Sad Sack,

the sky is flat.

All agog, apt adept. Whetted.

Precious angles between stapler, phone, and hole punch.

Today means ransack.

Cars carving snow squares.

Short shrift ties torn blouses. Thread the tightest fit.

Score an angle for the round-and-round.

Spare the molecular family, down the hall, love you all.

Voice is a rugged instrument, scratch as any hum.

Fast as a grope uphill. Deconstructing on the run.

Grace under pleasure. Poetics of hop and pop.

Impish ignition.

Lines across my inner city link in no way sure.

Kick out copy:

help these pages consume a little.

These days are the momentary lull.

Hatch spurs lately.

Serpentine.

Bent into glamour and seedy truncates.

Hum elastic slip thrashes.

This morning happened yesterday.

Scorning ornaments fourth in line.

Whirls tug at our centre. Flood and a moat.

Break and catch, breath and throat.

Does he scruple to break the seal?

– Anne Carson, *Eros the Bittersweet*

does he bother, does he whip. when and how. surely. fastened, does he. charmed. fathoming. he prevaricates, strung shoddy, panther, glam. how scruple. lip. how futile. part feathers out to. thins. he feathers out the thinnest. millimetrical. shaming. leaf print. oak storm. fly-leaf trace paper. scrawl all beckon. scruples portioning. drastic elements. division. how plausible. drafting. does he. strain. clatter clap shock. lidded. stirring. a quick drift. sheds over. nightly. does he. showering night might stunt. he scruples with blinkers. driven. dun. sheets over scrabbling. stun to break. shun to. break onto another's shores. a long shunted spell of. and shape to. grade sand to. shore breaking under wave. reforming wave. a shift. a sand pack. without scruple. or cram. sand under heel, does he. cram-packed. salted by wave and breaking. lustre. smoothing. lushest smooth shaping. to seal. to seal it with. lush smooth under. to shudder under wave. to seal without breaking. to sway.

I have not hauled this waxen heart /

from the gnarled bole of a great tree

– Lisa Robertson, *Debbie: An Epic*

Have not ever. Have not also. Hurt and heathered. Have not striven. Have not

groped. Have not sought value in ecstasy, surplus, and drain. Have not

parenthesized, obliquely, in taut horror.

In caressing, have not sampled. Have not surrounded, have lacked

caution, have not policed.

Having no pale feathering waste, have not tasted hail, have not

sanctioned or withered. Listening carelessly, with great signal tension, have

neither gleaned nor soothed. With open severing, slim reverence rooting itself,

with harsh squandered fluid esteem draping endlessly, have not scrawled vain

shapes or trills.

Have looted violets, have mortared sole.

I have and have not confidently corrupted my firm traction. And I have spoken eloquently shawled with rueing. I have plain humour capsized, enrapture stunned, slow salted leaking.

Shun routinely glamouring my affect, I have persisted in blame and ransom. I have held my heart crass, soft foam crashing my breakers.

Tasting lawless intrigue, have not rotted and have limberly skirted rain. Have woven hopelessly, simple desperate tremor trailing my fingers.

affect Thrum

We have floundered and basted. Our portions have multiplied. We are sated but repenting. We are lost to our innermost rhythm. Our senses are surfeit. Our form is buffeted.

A light pulse has led us sparing. We have not sought stability. Our uncertainty has charmed us. We are as a gluttonous lover. And yet we have been wrenched. We have contorted. We atone.

Flimsy surrendering baits us. Stubborn thickets spring to our mercy. Sabotage entices our lean baselessness. We hover fearing.

Our signal is a study in calm. Loop upon loop has cocooned. We have endeared ourselves to our other selves. Our clamour subsides. We are burgeoning.

We are no longer young in weather.

– Gertrude Stein, *History or Messages from History*

No longing. No weathering. No foot shod strung. No placid rashness. Shunning no policy of neglect, no rampant pander, no palaver, no claim. We have filed no strict revision, no order sorting us into sleeted or snowed in or resigning to.

We have elitely corseted our desires.

We have fondly drawn provision from placid calm erasing.

We have eroded intensely to concrete, to substructure's insistent pull. Goaded we have shed into other shells, collapsing borders. We stint no fluid, but pith and pulp evade craving.

We veer adrift, take shifting givens, and raid our own misgiving. Bloom or gather, we have weathered all ellipses. We start to elapse and traipse the hours, then flock to ruts, pander looming, foolishly humouring stun. Routinely we have treasured apparition, rating common trance as lucid strain. We have wafted cotton, adrift in tenured ribbing. We stray from random fathoming and fall into pollen's welt.

SMASH SWIZZLE FIZZ

pall mall caruso tom collins to the moon rum runner

apple river inner tube chelsea sidecar sloe driver

galactic ale kiss in the dark why not woodstock

zero mist banana slip stalactite lonely night

lebanese snow kokomo joe

look out below golden friendship hop toad

naked pretzel nijinski blini beer buster sloppy joe's

special rough gin squirt tequila collins fog cutter

gentle ben gauguin bloomsbury boomerang bay

city bomber alabama slammer

van vleet frisky witch cream fizz gin swizzle

kretchma cocktail ninotchka pavlova supreme

purple passion tea bull shot bolshoi punch banshee

fruity smash jack's jam manhasset narragansett

rory o'more

bermuda rose jamaica granito cara sposa bahama mama

bajito honolulu hula-hula hokkaido diabolo yolanda cuba

libre la jolla cocomacoque canado saludo sweet maria

caipirinha toreador tijuana taxi tequila mockingbird

rosita floridita viva villa joulouville

shavetail monkey shine shooter smooth move oh my

gosh between the sheets moon quake shake shady

lady champagne flamingo shalom cherie licorice mist

international incident depth bomb burgundy bishop

mont blanc montmartre albemarle fizz

SURGE

blurry moon

puzzles over

its tenure

sheds cumbersome

news, ferrets

urges from

loose garish

hair-swept

"Beware self-harvested shellfish"

Shale, fur, frailty. Harsh measures. Shards of shatter's after. Scattering apt travesties. Crawling opulent fifths.

Beware of harvesting self, root tug soil tumble, silent carrot scream, plug shock. Be leery, be lush.

Tassle shell, hardly. Fumbled, shun. False start wears thin. Vested interest sails through shades of horror's shipwreck. Shade yourself. Grow bleakly. Scan horizon for simple arrows. Eye the arc of night.

"Let's pander to our inner misgivings"

Let's atrophy brain-stem signals. It's our nature we abhor. It's only to flounder, reef, pluck.

I'd love to peel away from you, my open storm cellar, my rational ladder –

I'm certain of tragic consequence, of filling gaps with loose sand. No sand-packed ramming. Only shed gravelling. Only downslope escape.

"Earth to space station: dream"

Hurts to pace, hurts to siphon, peels to blinding glass. Refract amazement, but cautiously, cleverly. Take a step, ponder. Turn back to what elapsed. Carefully. Sift for treasure, caress. All we gather spills. All we grasp.

Sifting elation from hold to sense, from dream to palm to solid. To where you stand, what can you claim.

Rough cut slope dissects valley. Slight hills baring to dust. Scored hills bear their accumulation, their wear. Dun lines cut grass cover. Highway scores escape. Traversing still an echoing whine. Pitch your tragedies to a gentler slope. Proceed warily but wide. Horizon cracks your head butt cracks the horizon. The sky can't end. The sky can't press. You'll stand suspended under sky, of sky. You'll gel. You'll weather.

"Sexting to the wrong person"

We vex, we reason. Calibrate text to affect. Gag back vesting.

Ape throng.

An awesome looming storm cloud passes, no hassle, no dangerous song erupts, no drench, no furling verge. We rue, we zither. Attach to long shot lunging past. Let our humble sense last, carry errors to testing grounds, grave empathy exacting passion, burnt purpose, enact us.

Level stone, shape sediment ineffably fastened, hung chained. Risibly bordered by longing. Hemmed in with shuddering lust. We verge on loss. Correct we earn our pauses. Select our tense.

"Standoff ends with surrender"

Then who are we? Implacable stubborn underbelly sloughing itself daily.

Awkward portion of lust. What of our vibrating core? Stencils lend us shape but

no form, no presence, no protruding. We could not just as well. Could wither or

render. Spend or flop. What gales shape us wear out over seas, revert to circling

slow breezes, disappear into deep.

"Turns out humans can infect birds too"

Room to turn and procreate and lavish and hurt. Room to exonerate to honour.

First roots shoot and peck. First level, then harvest extends to humid fellows, assuming turns to burrowing. We get burnt. We set out and turn back extravagantly. Flaunt our corrections. Oscillate gravely.

What do we weather together? How blindly we wreck our nuisance. How erect our fumbling, how unfeathered we flail.

"Pushing hot border buttons"

What encumbers us? What heated guild hems? We're crumbling, we're bundled.

Assembling holiday memories for bargain-basement rent.

We're horror stories strut, haunted tension, hunt lushes.

We're rushing buttons to barter, crash standing. We're addled, sung sure, cradled,

rutted, and rung.

We're bottom hoarders, cling shuts. Crate sore.

"Satellite smash-up creates dangerous debris"

Some kind of dangerous dream marks you. The centre contains smashing. The outward thrust evaporates.

Reap, react. Desperate sanction. Grave flattery. Pull back slowly. Unfurl in measured pace. The outlines falter but never fade.

The machinery ululates. Uncover rotor. Calculate whirr.

Count down to stuttered rumblings. Dim brick crumbles into analogue torrents. Each blast of air rushes into its taut molecules too quick to trap.

"It's tradition but also"

throats in hands
memorize stitching
count all fingers, count toes

clamped down
lick your safety clean

across cityscape
on sidewalks, at traffic lights
shuttled, trap hemming

many hands
sugared numb
many throttlings

"A first they'd rather wasn't"

Orchestrate limp and slip oblique. Skate backwards. Rather flutter than stuff.
Rather roast than weigh. They'd fill themselves first. They'd take. Collate they.
Suture.

Bloom away from their conception, the space they fill sours. Interrogates
flippancy. Rates grain with false intention. Sluices pressure through gated
reserve.

"Female touch triggers risky decisions"

Rig up slippery levers. Pull up gunning for sight. Grip elision in finger pads, whorls of skin singe tight. Derail the sky, cloud dome, the singling burst, the crass chug, thunder grips deep into shuddering doubt.

Give over, stray. Give back delicate sifting. Late mazes. Ripples damping gaze. Drug to tumble. Shin tugged to reach.

ACKNOWLEDGEMENTS

Earlier versions of poems in this book have appeared in *Dusie*, *filling Station*, *NöD*, *Queen Street Quarterly*, *Post-Prairie: An Anthology of New Poetry*, Jon Paul Fiorentino and Robert Kroetsch, eds. (Talonbooks, 2005), *Shift & Switch: New Canadian Poetry*, Jason Christie, Angela Rawlings, and derek beaulieu, eds. (Mercury Press, 2005), *Shy: An Anthology*, Naomi K. Lewis and Rona Altrows, eds. (University of Alberta Press, 2013), and *The Best Canadian Poetry in English* 2013, Sue Goyette, ed. (Tightrope Books, 2013). Much gratitude to all the editors involved. Thank you to No press for the lovely chapbook edition of "Smash Swizzle Fizz." Many of these poems first appeared in chapbooks from my micro-press, edits all over.

I'm grateful to Daphne Marlatt and all the writers who attended Sage Hill in July 2010, and to the Alberta Foundation for the Arts for funding my attendance. Thank you to the Banff Centre for the Arts for supporting my self-directed writing residencies. Thank you to Garry Thomas Morse for putting this publication into motion, and to everyone at Talonbooks. Thank you to Marc Herman Lynch for insightful edits, and to all my friends and family for their support. Last but far from least, thank you to the members of the Natalie Simpson Writing Group for the Illiterate and Visually Impaired.

NATALIE SIMPSON

Natalie Simpson's poetry has appeared in several anthologies, including *Post-Prairie* (Talonbooks, 2005), *Shift & Switch* (Mercury Press, 2005), *Shy* (University of Alberta Press, 2013), and *The Best Canadian Poetry in English* 2013 (Tightrope, 2013). She practises pro bono law in Calgary, Alberta, and curates *filling Station* magazine's flywheel Reading Series. Her first book of poetry, *accrete or crumble*, was published by LINEbooks in 2006.